Meaning

Laura Lee

BookLeaf
Publishing

Presentation by *BookLeaf Publishing*

Web: www.bookleafpub.com

E-mail: info@bookleafpub.com

ISBN: 9789358317572

First edition 2023

*To my mother Cynthia and my children
Kaiden and Evelyn*

ACKNOWLEDGEMENT

The courage to take the step out to write things others could read would not have taken place nor would my life feel as vibrant, happy and full with out my sister Danielle, my dearest friends Emily, Justine, Michael all of whom continually encourage me to write and my beloved family. My parents and step parents instilled a love of culture, music, travel, connection and words that fuel my imagination continually.

PREFACE

A collection of musings and professions of love to the most meaningful people, places, and things in my life to date

Time Travel

Weighed down by the daily struggles
What it takes to simply survive
Tired of merely passing
A new hope to bloom and thrive

The pull is there to do better
But maybe for now that's simply to be
Not focused on here or there
I just breath then wait and see

Relax and just be present
Feel my weight upon the earth
And somewhere in the waiting
I find a brand new birth

I meet a little girl there
A younger bit of me
When I sit and listen
I feel lighter instantly

I listen to her stories
Of times when she felt wronged
Then I offer missing pieces
The things for which she longed

I promise I'll do better
I'll fight to have her back
Defend her and accept her
Give her all she felt she lacked

Kindness and attention
Acceptance and true love
Told her she was just right
Not too little or too much

I clean up thoughts that hurt her
And filled with empathy
I tell her I am sorry
For what I've done to me

The times I may have listened
To twisted views instead
Of things I truly knew were right
In our heart and in our head

I now walk a little surer
Ready to move ahead with Grace
 I've removed the negativity
From the sacred place

I leave the past behind me
The future yet to come
I'm living in the moment
Proud of what I've done

I can visit memories
And see clearly what I want
But neither place feels daunting

The core of the truth begins to unravel
Being present here and now is the true art of
time travel

Moving On

Now love here has manifested
All that I've hoped for has seemed to come
I've wished and prayed all my days
And I think that you may be the one

You knew before I knew
You said the very first moment we met
But it took me a while
Though I sure loved your style
To get past a mound of regret

I've fallen before for the wrong one
That had it all there on the outside
But under his charm came anger and harm
From the demons he managed to hide

Mistakes and misuse covered with papers and a
swiftly bought fake ring
But out of that mire life's greatest gift
Many lessons came tied with that string

But a string of two can unravel
When only one carries all of the hope
But I wouldn't have grown
Except for all that I've known

A desire to more than just cope

No ending is fully one sided
It takes two to tango for sure
But I can say I was the only one dancing
And that my intentions truly were pure

I know in the beginning
we all tend to put forward our best
But after years and confirmed fears
I was still here with all of the mess

We all seek what we were presented
Love looks like the model shown
So I sought a daily connection
And he sought a love of his own

I surely had intended
To take time to fully heal
And while I still do
I can do it with you
Working with the love that we feel

In every way that he hurt me
You love away all of the pain
In ways he made me feel broken
You say his loss is your gain

You said to me finders keepers

And truly make me feel seen
I listen to my heart now
And follow where I lean

While stories of pain can prepare us
Of how not to repeat the past
If we can stay with our minds in today
I know our story will last

Time to put down all that baggage
And truly work to forgive
So that you and I can do more than get by
We can thrive and live

We did more in just a few weekends
Than in decades of time before
It all seems to be there
When we lay our hearts bare
When we stand at the edge of the shore

All the things that we share in common
I've counted them here of late
Our minds seem one, our hearts aren't done
Healing to be our best mate

If I can clean up my messes
And you get out of your own way
When we take time to help the other
We can heal a little each day

The things that make us both thrive
We value above all else
We delve and grow and seek to know
The God within our self

We share a faith filled passion
Aligning with Gods perfect plan
Knowing God designs better
Than anything we can

I hoped and prayed
And would have stayed
Had he wanted me
But a cord of two would never do
You need a cord of three

Excited for the future
To step out in God's plan
Not just survive but truly thrive
And do life hand in hand

Major

The first one to love me
The first one to tell of God's love
The first one to make sure
We always had enough
She gives of her time when she'd rather be quiet
Full of grace
She smells like home
She shakes when she laughs and lights up the
room
She walks with God so she's never alone
Content in her room of prayer
But she ventures far from there
She brings your needs to God's ears
He answers most her prayers
Faithful
Weaving a legacy
Gods love flows through her
Through me
Onto my little one that looks like her
We walk down life's path
She's smaller now
I still look up to her somehow
Even as I wrap her in my arms
There's a rainbow on the ceiling
As we talk and cuddle close
We used to walk to see swans

Many things make me think of her
Butterflies make me think of her most
Her voice her wisdom her support
We didn't mesh when I was young
But when I had my own
I saw and understood a mother's love
Appreciation for all she did and does
I know time will take her
I can't imaging a world without her smell and
smile in it
I feel blessed to still have her for a while
But even when she goes
I'll feel her presence in flowers, swans,
butterflies and love
For today I'm glad I still have her voice
She asks how I am
I share
She listens
She tells me of her day
No talk feels small
My earliest memory climbing in her lap
Scratchy blue against my cheek from her
uniform
a Major lesson in priorities
The last cuddle under a Waterford lamp
An orb of light
When I count my blessings she's always at the
top
The first one to love me

Bestie

I saw her first once long ago
She was different like me
She went with the flow
We couldn't quite see
And we didn't know
That we would be that close
Through many versions of our self
Happy, sad, in sickness and health
Broke as a joke or wrapped up in wealth
She's been my ride or die
Her hair all those years ago in coils and curls
We cut and colored it different ways over
decades
A canvas of friendship filled with beautiful
painted photos and memories
Inside jokes, wondrous adventures, growth
My free spirit found a home alongside hers
She brought me gifts from across the world
I bought her a comfort blanket when life rained
down and ruined the one I gave her
A compass round her neck to remind her I'm the
direction she can go when she needs someone to
have her back
She has mine too, when life's delivered blows

I can call her and she knows just the sound of
her voice and the comfort of her grounds
When my eyes are closed and I'm seeking peace
and sparks of joy
So often it's thoughts of her alongside me
Glow worms and fjords, from the Prado to the
Louvre she met me or brought me from where I
was at to where I wanted to be
Blue roofs on white buildings walking along the
coast from places on bucket lists, graveyards and
planets found in countries I never would have
ventured to without her
Black beaches and floating ice, green lights
across skies, warm sangria under Spanish sun
So many of the best adventures and I know
we're nowhere near done
She's in a different season now, one I long since
passed through
There's new distance and challenges in our lives
But I'll call her later and check in to hear how
she is feeling as she's growing another part of
her life
I'm not sure she knows what her friendship
means to me
That in a world that was hard she felt so easy to
know and love
We are both wanderers and the world is better
with her in it

She's a sister I chose, my very favorite travel
buddy, a safe exciting soul, such a juvenile
nickname but we met in our teens so still
halfway through life and forever I'll call her
bestie

Story Weaver

Like a missing puzzle piece she came along and
fit with ease
Our quirks and love of books that bond us
Feeling instant kinship and trust
Like family but closer
Life is better with her in it
Story weaver
I could listen to her forever
She's beautiful inside and out
A sassy intellect
And yet
Sweet innocence combined
Green eyes
Wide hips
Full and lovely lips
If she weren't taken I think I'd maybe try
But I know part of her heart is mine
As part of mine is hers
We roll around on the waters edge
Swim in fjords and climb up hills
We talk for hours and split our food
Story weaver
She feels like a missing piece to my soul
Viking sister
You made me feel whole
I can't imagine life without you now
It's hard to believe it's just half a decade

But what a true deep friendship we have made
With lots more life and adventures to share
I can wonder out loud with you
I can be myself with you
You can wander about with me
You can know that I'll be true
A walking glimmer half a world away
Part of my hearts in the next day
Your voice is my favorite
Sharing adventures
Story weaver
You're my bosom friend
When I'm not quite sure in life
And need some clarity
A compass, a dictionary
She's perfect as she is
Even when she responds
but then forgets to send
Story weaver
I know we'll catch each other eventually
A world away a part of me
A small name but of such great importance
Im sorting my life out
And counting the days
Until I see her again
She writes worlds
And is a favorite part of mine
I miss you
Story weaver

Good one

Cuddling a hoodie
Smelling a rose
Looking at a photo
Reading a note
in the hand written card that you wrote
How can you not know that you're a good one

Walking on the beach
Talking heart to heart
I miss you from the moment
That we are apart
How can you not know you're a good one

From our deep connection
To you your ever changing eyes
I'm not used to someone
Who isn't versed in lies
How can you not know that you're a good one

I've said all I can say
3 little words and 100s more
I've never bonded with another man
Or maybe never wanted to before
How can you not know that you're a good one

So much the same in all we think and do
You're so quick to see and love me
Well I feel the same for you
It is so far past the time that you start to too
Honey please believe that you're a good one

So full of wisdom
So full of wit
I will take you all
What I see is what I get
From one liners to drawn out tales
I'll take you as you are
You're one of the good ones

Us

Created in your image
What did us really mean
I guess the truth is in us all
And still remains to be seen

If god in their image made man
and then from a rib woman grew
Perhaps at the heart of it
God I think may be a woman too

A group of men decided what books would
make it in
Then added up the rules and made us feel like it
was sin
Control the population
Was it divine intervention?
Why did Mary barely make it
Why do we use it to judge
Only Jesus was perfect
And all He did was love

Jesus Christ the savior now used as a swear
If you listen for it, it's thrown round everywhere
Religion, politics polarizing divides

Keep us busy and distracted and behind it truth
hides
If we all realized we are all just only human but
also part of God
I see God in you

Labels divide I understand wanting to proudly
stand after history hid you in the shadows but
categories just further separate
we are the same
little boy turned little girl with help of knives
and pills
Slipping farther from each other hate that slowly
kills
You can sit in the stall beside me
Go where you feel safe
If it is harming no else and you can look you in
the face
I will be a safe place I see God in you

I told a sister in Christ about abuse and misuse at
home
And she said that she would pray for me
I only felt more alone
Divorce is a sin
So is judgement and hatred sewn
I can forgive
I see God in you

It's getting easier to simply be alone
Just me and my maker
People are hard and they hurt
But we all need connection
That's why we are here
To love
It hurts to love
Turn the cheek when you are hit and hated
Until you've had enough
God puts the lonely in families
Mine is broken up
I can't take that anymore
I forgive and will always love
I see God in him

Searching for fulfillment and purpose
Homeless people I feed and serve
I take time to listen and see
There looking over their shoulders
I see God in me

Sister sister

The only constant in childhood years
Also the cause of some of my tears
No one else could hurt me but you could
You also made me feel safe like no one else on
Earth

You see the weave of the tapestry of what makes
someone who and what they are and you could
always find the one string to pull to tear it apart
and rip out a heart
Swipe out legs

You don't use that gift like that anymore
You find the strings and weave them with gold
to make people feel stronger in their weaknesses
and heal

I'm so glad you're mine
Sister sister
We walked hand in hand
Through fields in lands near and far

Barking dogs and gliding swans
Fear and beauty
You were the one constant

Magic memories of dancing by ruins
Looking at Elven doors
You scared me and made me safe

We talk weekly
Your hugs are home though
You're too far away
I count the days

Your voice grounds
Your wisdom and knowledge
Direct
You are the color of November 9th
Fall leaves and purple

There's safety in your voice
And home found in your arms

Baggage

He beamed when I told him he hurt me
What sort of man does that
And despite what you say, he'll have his way
When he makes his way up to bat

Perpetual boundary crosser
A bully down at his core
He pushed and he yelled with threats thinly
veiled
Until the day he walked out the door

I know it takes two to argue
I surely have my faults too
But I did the work to be less of a jerk
So in the end I'm glad that we're through

The hard part is I still love him
And I'm doing the work to forgive
But when I was quickly replaced with a prettier
face
It makes it harder to live

I wish I could turn it all off now
The memories of the abuse
But my biggest fear is with all the kids hear

That they will turn out just like you

I'm not trying to paint you a villain
You have good qualities too for sure
But at the end of the day, I can sure say
That my intentions were pure

I feel I put in the effort
To try and thrive in the role
I read every book and mastered the look
And all I lost was my soul

So now our lives are separate
Except where the kids are involved
We're not the same, we're on different planes
One of us evolved

Healthy and unhealthy
Simply can not coincide
So when you're at you height and just want to
fight
I go for flight and hide

I'll call one of my people
And vent about how it's no way to live
But I'm tired now, so want to put it all down
And truly work to forgive

I can with all assurance

Say I truly wish you the best
If not for you, then for those two
So I will pray and I leave the rest

Im putting down the baggage
It's too much to have and to hold
Irreconcilable we say, you'll be bitter but pay
All we had divined or sold

I'll hope one day for closure
That a friendship could start to grow
Maybe you'll one day find, what it takes to be
kind
I guess with time we will know

Girl

Freckles like stars in the sky
I wish only good for her
My love for her like her eyes
Deep and beautiful

What the world will make of her
Amber gold and green
My goal is to build her up
Know I'm a place she can be safely seen

If I could I would protect her
But the world will subject her to pain
Whispering in her ear
She should be this way

My job to love and mold her
Correct her wrongs when I can
But to let her be what God made her to be
Walking hand in hand

So at home in a city
Shopping on rue Tiphaine
If I could only give her everything
And keep her from feeling pain

Somewhere in between woman and girl
Growing into who she is
If I could I'd give her the world
There's no roll greater than this

We come from a long line of women
Strong, a little crazy, messy but kind
I wonder what beyond those molds
Authentically she'll find

If we all try a little harder
To be better than what came before
To outgrow the limitations
Of generations keeping score

I wish I could've done better
To clean a bit more of the mess
But where it really counts I think she'll prove
That she can pass the test

At the end of the day I'll model love
With kindness accept who she'll be
I'll share openly and deeply
When she asks for tea

Maybe others will judge our friendship
Say it's not my job to be that
But I love that she knows
Here as she grows home is where I'm at

I'll buy her bits and pieces
But hope at the end of the day
There's more value in love than all the stuff
More meaning in words we say

Such different things will be modeled
From different sides of the street
But somewhere between our girl will grow
And in the middle she'll meet

I worry where we let her down
But hope God Will compensate
What happens when one models love
But the other shows anger and hate

She'll have conflicting stories
But from both sides she's given love
So in the areas we failed her
I hope she'll rise above

Maybe prayers will be answered
Then one day time will find
She has all my heart and creativity
All his sharpness and his mind

She's fierce and fiery
Spicy, bold but sweet
She's making her own way

Though everything but neat

But amongst the trail of messes
There's beauty in her path
So much love and joy she brings
I hope the closeness lasts

I worry her need for attention
There's likely some damage there
I hope in the time I give her
She knows that I love her and care

There's not much I wouldn't give her
When she hurts my heart it breaks too
I hope that she sees she's more than a shell
And she sees my point of view

The outside for sure is gorgeous
But so is her mind and heart
In a world of fake phony copies
She's a priceless work of art

Surely the most beautiful thing
I ever created grew or made
I hope and pray a legacy of love
Will continue and never fade

I still see her little in my mind sometimes
There's battles yet to be fought

But I'll try my best to model Grace
And never force her to be what she's not

And as I mark her growth
In stature and height I'll see
One day wishes and prayers will be answered
She'll go farther and higher than me

Step

I think it means more
You didn't have to love but you did
You saw a need and met it
No greater act of service shown
So often made to feel like too much
He simply smiled and said sweetie beetie
So many words of wisdom and phrases
So many lessons modeled and shown
When I seek to find areas that I'm proud of
 I know he helped me grow
Have I told you lately?
The answer is always yes
You wrapped us in words of encouragement
Teaching lessons of how to make sense
Generosity and sharing
So many things that give life meaning,
You the greatest model
Culture and class
Hard work
You helped make dreams come true
Walking on antique ships making history come
to life
The gifts of other cultures
What valuable lessons
You foster, saved and support all that is dearest

Even in the few darker moments of anger,
promises were kept modeling God's love once
again
You were something wholly different
Not afraid to feel and show
Sipping scotch or brandy
Moving pieces with another soon to be eagle
I know none of us would soar near as high
Had you not chosen to love
I'm so grateful
For this step
It surely lifted us all up

Lessons

Summertime memories
Barefoot camping
Skipping showers to swim
Diving for keys and cans
Fun found outside and in
She instilled my love of learning
Gave the gift of word
Knew and grew every flower
He spotted every bird
Compassion, follow your passion, creativity
Hard work and nature walks
Inappropriate movies
The love of deeper talks
Digging for letters
To build the best word
His piano playing
The best sounds ever heard
It sounds of home and blues
Billy, Elton and Daddy too
Stage presence, that juggling clown
You were the best when you were around
But a world away in a different town
We visit when we can
1 flavor ice cream stand
She taught me the difference I or me

She doesn't talk much but there's not much she
can't see
Perfect lotioned hands
Petite freckled tan
Shocked me with the lesson
you don't need a man
Harmonica playing
One man band
I went on stage for you
Through the fear I grew
Two jobs and a bike
Through the woods we hike
Drifting on the water
I know I am your daughter
You make people feels seen
You make everyone smile
We don't talk as much I know it's been a while
We maybe see different versions still
But talk every so often when there's time to kill
Truly some of the greatest lessons were taught
by you
Square knots, shoot straight, treasure hunting
parallel parking, cooking
Find beauty in everyone you see
I find much of you when I look at me
Creativity fostered
I try to make others smile and feel seen
I search for rocks and stars
Seniors and special needs

Giving happiness is the greatest of the deeds
And I see magic in the world
That you painted for me
You also taught me if you aren't happy
Leave

Prices

Prices
Proud of this clan
Cardinal rules
He called me doll and owned oranges
She smiled and was Hope
He played the violin London man
She made movies and is bold
He danced around the world
She saw the future with scary accuracy
He managed so much so well on stage and off
We drove across country and danced in canyons
had laughs deeper still
She prayed attention and said awoman
She taught me let go and lean in
He listens and says here is the best place
She smiled and smelled ghosts
He flies in the air
She just seems the the coolest
He is stoic and great with investments
She sat with powerful politicians
I don't know all their story and can count on one
hand how many times I've met them most over a
whole life but they are mine and I am theirs and
every time I learn something else
I feel proud to boast

This clan
I wasn't born into it
But grateful I now am

Sweater

The crest on the chest
of the sweater you left
Reminders of what you've done
You opened my heart
But now we're apart
We're past the days of fun
I'm staring at my phone
On the cover
Two feet entwined at sunrise
by the shore on which
We walked before
by moonlight
We talk each day
We share and pray
You saw a future
I was a few chapters behind
The pages from floor to ceilings
There's holes in the story
Red flags and green ones mix
Brown is the binding of the book
you bought for me
I think with time
Our pieces could be fixed
But let's take it slow

see where we go
We share meals
Our minds our hearts
we cuddle and walk
in my kitchen we kiss
I don't know what it is
But I want more of this
We flew away after moonlit walks
Another city's pavement took our feet
All the things we wanted to find in love
We find in each other
You ask to hear the words
Before our bodies meet
We dance and sway to the piano man and his
uptown beat
Things get real when we get back
You're too focused on things you lack
Slippery downward spirals
But you can ride for miles
So get back in the saddle again
You saw and said all you needed to
I open all my pages
You cracked the code
You read me like a book
You asked me what it meant
my deep and troubled look
I have so many layers of fear
Intermingled past and present and future
All coming clear

The reason I am here
Love
I feel that for you
You promised you wouldn't hurt me
you said you really do all you say
that you'll always come through
You said your love doesn't change
To the moon and back
But I feel it wax and wane
when you get in your own way
Are we at the beginning still or maybe the
middle, or nearing the end?
There's no measure on our pages
No sure fire gauges
You said you understood and see me
like a bird flying free you'd let me be me
you would love me, and hope that I would come
back to the aviary
You keep feeding me bread
I'm not sure it's good for me
But like all your words of love
I swallow it all anyway
The love we share feels rare
Meeting on all planes
Except where egos matter
We really are the same
You painted a future
so brilliant and bright
I was captivated by the thought

When we lay on leather
I'm only present
Nowhere that I'm not
Then away from you
My mind wanders again
I think she's poison
Every time you go back to her
Sweet pet names cooked meals
Her big home has part of you
And when you sleep under the roof
You feel small
You spiral there and I can't pull you out
You push me away
Saying you want me always
Everyday my whole self
But guess you meant not through your sickness
and only if in wealth
And maybe two days from now you'll be back to
those words when you're back in health
I want all of them
Every inch of you
The spots like stars in the sky
I'm praying and wishing upon them
that you'll be fine
You're needed now
You saw me and told me so
You said a lot of things
Your feelings only grow
So why am I alone

It faintly smells of you
A shell you once wore
I wrap the empty sleeves around me
Are your promises empty too?
I could be your greatest love
3rd time is the charm
But only if we're good
We've both had more than enough harm
Tears on the crest in the center of the chest
Of the sweater that you left
Wondering how our story ends
41 years from now when I've had half your life
Sparkling blue ring marking me your wife
Or faded pages from a discarded chapter as we
both go on our ways
Makeshift empty shells
Can't love me half as well
50% isn't close
But I'd follow you to the ends of the earth
And you said to the moon and back
So please honey think on what you have
Not only what you lack
I'll wait until I'm in your arms again but for now
I'll close my eyes and dream of the man that
filled me, my heart and this sweater

Red

We met in an interesting chapter
I needed to put some fires out
We swam in water by water
You didn't cross the line
I felt instantly comfortable there
Photos from around the world
Stories so quick to share
Laying on lounges
Soaking up sun
Your skin is going red
Matching your flags
 But your ideas hold wisdom
Your stories and you as a whole
Dynamic and fun
Laughter is the best medicine
But I don't think you're the one
You share your drink
Your sun glasses
Your amusing stories
You feed me foods I enjoy
You're the oldest little boy
Wise and shrewd
The games begin
You treat me like a toy
But we enjoy each other's company for now

You respect my boundaries
But flirt with the line
We glide over waves and clouds
You tell me I'm being too loud
I shouldn't even try if there are knots to tie
I won't do it right
You show me to your friends
But that's where commitment ends
We are a world away from each other
We want very different things
Too much baggage on either end
And neither wanting strings
It was exciting while it lasted
But tainted looking back
You would work your way right through me
I wasn't ready for that
I was seeking friendship
You were wanting more
But I liked the way I didn't knock
And would walk right in your door
You saved me from being lonely
I saved your Mom's stuff on the floor
Broken pipes
Broken trust
You're waterfront home and tears
Causing damage and rust
I brought you gifts and coffee
You brought me laughter and pain

It's clearer now why no other woman has taken
your last name
Rojo flags, potent smelling fridge and sunset
Just when I'm over it
You say you'd like to see me
But we have no plans yet
And doubt we ever will
I've moved on to someone steady
His love is constant and makes me ready
I tell you, laying my plan bare
I'd like to be friends
You say we are friends
You say it's an overshare
You don't want to know my personal life
You don't really care
But then a few days later
You're right back there
Asking for my time
I say yes knowing we will both be too busy
But the up and down spinning round
Is making me too dizzy
You feel like him now
A part of my past
I like rereading books though
So who knows maybe I'll visit your page
If the self destruct button needs wrapping
It's red too
Like my blood I shed
And all of your flags

I tore out some pages
On to better stages
Rojo
Adios

Loupe

I see the red flags blazing
Waving in the wind
But there right along side them
Are green flags blending in

Maybe that's how life works
The good comes with the bad
Not sure if we will keep it
But it's the best we've ever had

I think when we're together
It all makes perfect sense
But then when life puts distance there
The trouble feels too dense

I know it's just a season
You pouring into her
And all the things you spoke of
Could maybe be my cure

I guess that I believe you
But you've said it all before
Maybe I'm just hopeful
You feel it this time more

Loving me is easy
At least that's what you said
But when you're gone I'm left alone
With thoughts inside my head

For all that sparkles isn't real
Some gems and words are fake
Really only time will show
If you keep the word you make

You show up strong and valiant
And chase my fears away
When thoughts you'll leave come creeping in
You assure me that you'll stay

But then some darker days
Seem to come about
And in your gloomy moments
I'm sometimes filled with doubt

It's isn't that you're worn down
I can handle when life's tough
It's that I start to feel
That I may not be enough

When you say you love me
Then show up every time
You seem to be a safe place
To keep this heart of mine

One day you may kneel before me
And say you'll take a vow
But I won't worry for the future
I'll just be here and now

I know that in the moment
I've felt safer there with you
Than any other man
And what they put me through

I feel that you'd slay dragons
That stood within my way
But more than that you've shown up
In the day to day

I tried to keep my walls up
But they came tumbling down
You make me feel protected
When you are around

The back and forward
Up and down
The riptide warning
Won't drag me down

The times we have been swimming
waters rough and tall in the sea

in well over our heads
you stood your ground by me

I think my biggest issue
Seems harder than the rest
Is despite the situation
I'll look for all the best

I see the things you painted
So clearly in my mind
I guess I'll have to wait and see
If it's what we will find

Somehow I have managed
To keep my soul still pure
I've seen my share of heartbreak
So wish I could be sure

The others here that know me
Have different things to say
But none of them are vested
Or will ever have to pay

I guess I'll weigh the outcomes
But see what I will find
I'll listen louder with my heart
Than following my mind

All the things you tell me

That you say you'll do
I'll hope and pray that one day
They will all be true

And despite my reservations
In the moment it feels right
So I will just go with the flow
Won't live in fear and fight

Sure there's something scary
In giving love away
With no guarantee
The recipient will stay

But without a doubt one thing I know
The good outweighs the bad
We laugh and live, love and learn
We're the best we've ever had

So I will just watch closely
And study all of you
And hope that they are diamonds
The things you say you'll do

Strong, hard withstanding
Refined over time
Brilliant shining bright
This flawless love of mine

Something Else

You're too much
That's something I was often told
But the words that they put on me
feel worn out an old
I realize I'm really not
I have found what I sought
And for the right people
I am just the right amount
You'll never be right for the wrong ones
Too messy, too crazy, too loud
I will come at life authentically
show up myself and feel proud
If you change who you are to fit in
To somehow fit a mold
You're only fake and what's that take
To swap out tin for gold
In a herd with billions of copies
All dressed and sounding the same
How's it feel to just be real
Think back to how you came
Before you were taught
To be quiet and sit still
Before it was modeled
It's not ok to feel
Before you changed to fit in

And liked what they said you should
Before you stripped away passion
To just be labeled good
When you were maybe carefree
In your younger days
Think of how it felt
To revel in your ways
To dance like no one's watching
To see with open eyes
To show up as your true self
Wearing no disguise
That's the you I'd love to meet
The world needs more of that
But if you are not there yet
I'll meet you where you're at
Somewhere in acceptance
You'll feel more truly you
Knowing I'm a safe place
And hold a different view
I notice when I hold space
And simply let things be
All the things I'm meant for
Flow straight there to me
I will not judge your journey
I'd love to know your self
I will simply love and smile
And know we're something else

Bubba Face

Calm and kind
Wise beyond your years
You see moving pieces
 But amber eyes brim with tears
You are contained and quiet
Left to you your own devices
But when you laugh and smile
It lights up my whole world
Though less than planned
I prayed for you
The second I knew you were growing
I felt excitement and peace
Knowing despite the pain that put you there
I'd be blessed with life
When you're happy I'm happy
You are so aware of moods
You're guarded in solitude
But you'll let me in your room
Comma dot dot comma
A language of our own
I'm so proud of all you're doing
Can't believe how much you've grown
I look up to you on so many levels
You're the kindest hearted angel
In a world full of devils

You bring peace
I think back to younger days
Mirrored eyes and piercing cries
I was supposed to keep you safe
 and I've done my best to try
but when you hurt I hurt too
I hate to see you cry
Bubba face
What a silly little name I gave
To the best thing I've ever made
For one so serious beyond his years
Old soul
Bright mind
Best of humans
Caring and kind
You bring pride and joy
Beautiful clever boy
You're growing to a man
Not many could get through to you
Im glad that I still can
You're the best of humans
In a tiring place
Im glad I'm yours
And that your mine
My sweetest bubba face

Divorce

A bed the size for a king
But on one side alone sleeps a queen
If we'd stayed for all the wrong reasons
Wasting the rest of our seasons
What would it truly mean

Not every moment was bad
If I go traveling in my mind
There was laughter and care
When you were there
But peace we could never find

My messes and your anger
We sent each other up walls
Maybe your biggest goal
Was really utter control
What happens when only one falls

We made the two greatest treasures
And some wonderful memories
At the end of the day
We both had to pay
I'd like you to leave the keys

Taking the very last remnants

Of all that made me feel safe
You've done it before
You're yelling once more
Angrily in my face

This time in front of the children
Ranting and raving again
My biggest haunt
Is what they will want
Surrounded by angry men

It's time for us to do better
Take the space and time to heal
Work to forgive
So in peace we can live
Sort through all that we feel

Thinking back upon our journey
The places that we went
But we weren't for each other
You can't be great lovers
If all your energy is spent

I felt your daily resentment
No doubt you felt mine too
We both felt trapped
All attempts were tapped
Our love it poured right through

That isn't to say we didn't show it
Just in completely different ways
But the other never heeded
What we truly needed
Which is how a bond decays

I can say I put forward the effort
Praying and reading the book
Begging for help
But I'm alone by myself
Healing from what you took

Maybe with time we'll move forward
I can truly say I want the best for you
Build a friendship of sorts
No more angry retorts
Maybe you'll want what's best for me too

There for sure are certain aspects
That I will likely always miss
You could fix anything
Except what's bound with a ring
But I'll still think on your kiss

If we both tried harder to make it
We'd have become something we're not
At the end of the day
That's too much to pay
We'll be happy with what we've got

You've found someone who cleans better
I've found someone who is kind
It didn't take long
For each other we're wrong
Better suited was easy to find

So now as a chapter closes
And I process the path that we cross
We really weren't it
A very good fit
But we still both count it a loss

I'll try not to view the time wasted
There's so many lessons there
The memories haunt
And show what I want
A life filled with love and care

Someone who speaks our language
And values the same things that we do
Now that I've grown
I'm better alone
Than chasing and begging for you

So we say irreconcilable differences
And wait while the judge decides
I'll let it show

The pain that I know
You'll be the one that hides

Printed in the USA
CPSIA information can be obtained
at www.ICGtesting.com
LVHW011721090324
774045LV00005B/954